DETAILED GUIDANCE FOR ISSUING GREEN BONDS IN DEVELOPING COUNTRIES

DECEMBER 2021

ASIAN DEVELOPMENT BANK

ADB

Contents

Table, Figures, and Boxes

Acknowledgments

The Asian Development Bank (ADB) is collaborating closely with the Association of Southeast Asian Nations (ASEAN), the People's Republic of China, Japan, and the Republic of Korea—collectively known as ASEAN+3—to promote the development of local currency bond markets and regional bond market integration through the Asian Bond Markets Initiative (ABMI). ABMI was established in 2002 to bolster the regional financial system's resilience by developing local currency bond markets as an alternative source to foreign currency-denominated, short-term bank loans for long-term investment financing.

Detailed Guidance for Issuing Green Bonds was developed in accordance with the *ABMI Medium-Term Road Map, 2019–2022*, which was endorsed at the 22nd ASEAN+3 Finance Ministers and Central Bank Governors Meeting in 2018. The road map called for increased support for the development of the green bond market for infrastructure investment in ASEAN+3. This report was undertaken through ADB technical assistance on Creating Ecosystems for Green Local Currency Bonds for Infrastructure Development in ASEAN+3 and financially supported by the Government of the People's Republic of China.

This guidance note was prepared by Rob Fowler under the direction of Kosintr Puongsophol, financial sector specialist, Economic Research and Regional Cooperation Department (ERCD). Special thanks to the following staff for their advice and comments: Satoru Yamadera, advisor, ERCD; Shu Tian, economist, ERCD; Richard Supangan, senior economics officer, ERCD; Oth Marulou M. Gagni, senior operations assistant, ERCD; Alita Lestor and Yvonne Osonia, ADB consultants.

Abbreviations

ABMI	Asian Bond Markets Initiative
ADB	Asian Development Bank
ASEAN	Association of Southeast Asian Nations
ASEAN+3	ASEAN plus the People's Republic of China, Japan, and the Republic of Korea
CBI	Climate Bonds Initiative
ESG	environmental, social, and governance
EU	European Union
GHG	greenhouse gas
PRC	People's Republic of China

Introduction

The green bond market in ASEAN+3 has expanded tremendously in recent years.[1] The People's Republic of China (PRC) has the largest green bond market in ASEAN+3 and is home to one of the world's largest markets. Green bonds issued by PRC-based issuers totaled more than $22 billion in the first half of 2021, with nearly 100 transactions, followed by the Republic of Korea and Japan.[2]

Simultaneously, ASEAN members have made significant progress in developing domestic sustainable capital markets. Numerous initiatives have already been implemented by ASEAN governments, including the adoption of the ASEAN Green, Social, and Sustainability Bond Standards, as well as other significant initiatives such as the adoption of the ASEAN Capital Markets Forum's (ACMF) strategic directions for developing ASEAN sustainable capital markets and the ASEAN Taxonomy for Sustainable Finance.

Since the introduction of ASEAN Green, Social, and Sustainability Bond Standards by the ACMF in 2017, green, social, and sustainability bond issuance—all of which has been based on a use-of-proceeds approach— has grown rapidly among ASEAN issuers as they seek direct financing to fund investments in response to long-term environmental and social challenges. As of September 2021, the cumulative value of ASEAN-labeled green, social, and sustainability bonds had reached $16.4 billion (Figures 1 and 2).[3]

Figure 1: Issuance of ASEAN-Labeled Bonds by Country (USD million)

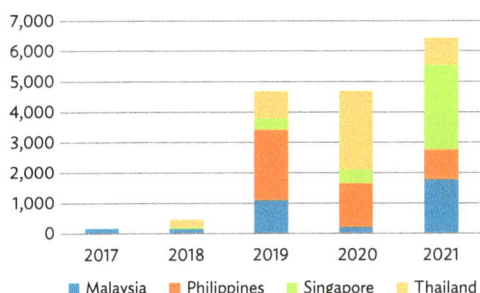

Figure 2: Issuance of ASEAN-Labeled Bonds by Category (USD million)

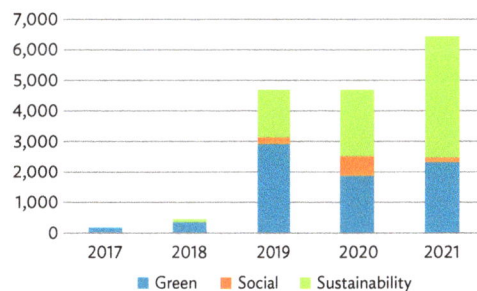

Sources: Securities and Exchange Commission, Philippines; and Association of Southeast Asian Nations (ASEAN) Capital Markets Forum.

---

[1] ASEAN+3 comprises the members of the Association of Southeast Asian Nations (ASEAN) plus Japan, the People's Republic of China, and the Republic of Korea.

[2] Climate Bonds Initiative. 2021. Sustainable Debt Market H1 2021. https://www.climatebonds.ent/files/bi_susdebtsum_h12021_02b.pdf.

[3] Securities and Exchange Commission, Philippines. Sustainable Finance Market Update. https://www.sec.gov.ph/investors-education-and-information/sustainable-finance-market-update/.

Building on this recent growth, ASEAN has significant opportunities to expand its sustainable finance markets, as well as for private sector issuers to incorporate environmental, social, and governance (ESG) considerations into their operations. It is also critical to simultaneously strengthen the capacity of capital market intermediaries to expand the pool of talent in this area. As a result, the Asian Development Bank (ADB) has prepared this guidance note to assist corporate bond issuers and their advisors to understand the process and key considerations for a successful green bond issuance.

About This Guidance Note

This detailed guidance note was created to assist bond issuers and their advisors to understand the process and key considerations for a successful green bond issuance.

Demand for green bonds and other sustainable finance products is increasing rapidly. Issuers are seeing an opportunity to be part of the green bond market, but are often not sure about how it works, what they need to do, and the key decisions to be made along the way.

The guidance note covers all of the steps required to follow best practices in labeling bonds as green. The sections on each step include relevant examples, links to further details, and key resources for green bond issuers and their deal teams (Figure 3).

Outline of the Labeling Process

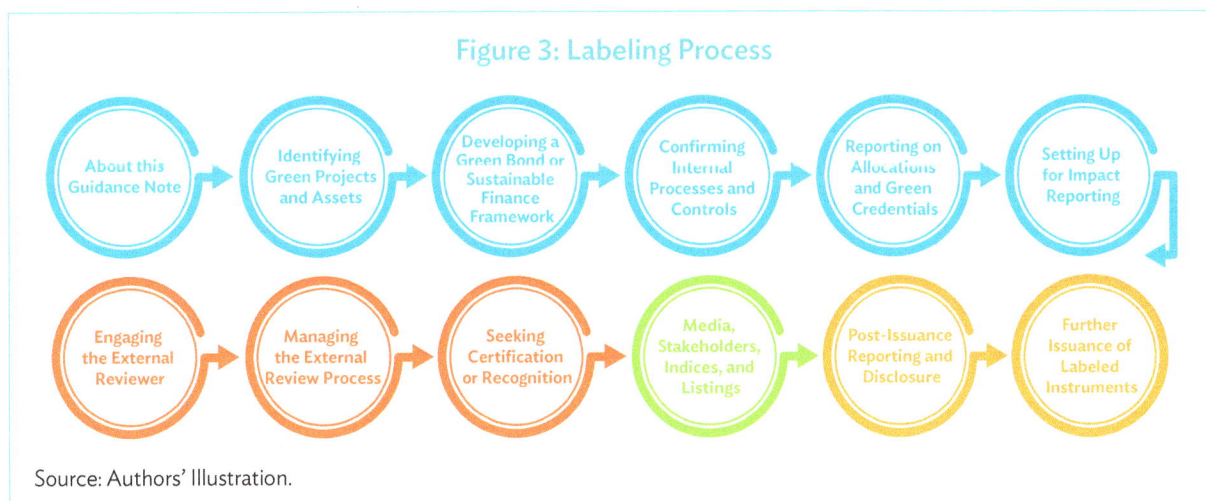

Figure 3: Labeling Process

About this Guidance Note → Identifying Green Projects and Assets → Developing a Green Bond or Sustainable Finance Framework → Confirming Internal Processes and Controls → Reporting on Allocations and Green Credentials → Setting Up for Impact Reporting

Engaging the External Reviewer → Managing the External Review Process → Seeking Certification or Recognition → Media, Stakeholders, Indices, and Listings → Post-Issuance Reporting and Disclosure → Further Issuance of Labeled Instruments

Source: Authors' Illustration.

There is often confusion among issuers and advisors on the differences between a sustainability bond and a sustainability-linked bond. It is important to clarify the use-of-proceeds model compared to sustainability-linked arrangements, as this guidance note only covers the use-of-proceeds model.

There are currently two major approaches to identifying bonds and debt instruments as having positive green or sustainability value. Green bonds, climate bonds, social bonds, and sustainability bonds all rely on the use-of-proceeds approach. This is the most common approach used by bond issuers. It identifies specific green projects, assets, and expenditures that are associated with the green bond.

Recently, there has been a surge in the alternative approach, which links sustainability outcomes for the bond issuer to the amount of interest (coupon rate) that is paid to investors. This usually involves a step-up or step-down in coupon rates triggered by the achievement (or not) of specific sustainability targets.

1. **Use-of-proceeds approach.** Per the Green Bond Principles, this refers to "any type of bond instrument where the proceeds will be exclusively applied to finance or re-finance, in part or in full, new and/or existing eligible green projects, assets, and expenditures, and which are aligned with the four core components of the Green Bond Principles."

2. **Sustainability-linked approach.** Per the Sustainability-Linked Bond Principles, this refers to "any type of bond instrument for which the financial and/or structural characteristics can vary depending on whether the issuer achieves predefined sustainability or (environmental, social, or governance) objectives. In that sense, issuers are thereby committing explicitly (including in the bond documentation) to future improvements in sustainability outcome(s) within a predefined timeline. Sustainability-linked bonds are a forward-looking, performance-based instrument and are aligned with the Sustainability-Linked Bond Principles."

Two Parallel Tracks

There are two tracks of work to consider when labeling a bond, loan, or *sukuk* (Islamic bond) as "green." These two tracks are equally important to investors when they are considering the labeled investment.

The first track is for the eligibility of the projects, assets, and expenditures. This involves the issuer demonstrating that the projects, assets, and expenditures associated with the green bond are aligned with a set of green definitions, or a "taxonomy." Selecting which taxonomy to use, or when not to use one, is described in Identifying Green Projects, Assets, and Expenditures.

The second track is for the integrity of the issuer's internal systems and controls when it comes to the processes involved in labeling a bond. This includes procedures and governance for selecting green projects, assets, and expenditures; management of the bond proceeds; and regular reporting and disclosure in line with the issuer's Green Bond Framework.

The guidance note highlights best practices for both of the abovementioned tracks. Issuers can achieve best practices in the second track of work, no matter which green definitions are used. These internal systems and controls can support a broad range of labeling activities for an issuer (e.g., green, social, or sustainable).

The First Time Is Challenging but Worth It

Issuers of green bonds have described the extra effort required for labeling as being significant for the first labeled transaction but much less so for future activities. Subsequent green transactions use the same Green Bond Framework, internal processes, and controls and tracking of proceeds as for the first green transaction, so it is much easier and faster compared to the first time (Box 1).

Treasurers from green bond issuers have described their strong intention to issue further green and labeled debt instruments, even though there was extra effort required to label the first transaction.

There are substantial benefits for green bond issuers if they can be the first to issue a green bond in a particular jurisdiction or a new sector, or by using a new structure. This amplifies the potential for the green bond to provide positive momentum for the issuer's sustainability credentials.

Box 1: Experience of BTS Group Holdings PCL, a regular green bond issuer from Thailand

BTS Group's second series of green bonds issued in November 2020 with 3.3x oversubscription indicated investors' confidence and goodwill towards the company and our green projects. On the back of strong demand, BTS Group decided to exercise the THB3,600 million greenshoe option, bringing the total issue size to THB8,600 million. The proceeds will be used to fund two new monorail projects (Pink line: 34.5 kilometers, Yellow line: 30.5 kilometers) in Bangkok, which are targeted to operate during 2021–2022. Both are anchored projects that will elevate Bangkok's electric mass transit network that will lessen the use of fossil-fueled vehicles, resulting in the reduction of carbon emissions and fine dust particles in the Bangkok metropolitan area. It is estimated that both projects will help reduce carbon dioxide emissions by 28,000 tons per year and will play an important role in bringing cleaner air quality to the city. Although issuing a green bond required additional work and resources to comply with our Green Bond Framework, we felt it is truly worthwhile. It is also worth mentioning that since this is our second issuance, our team had quite a steep learning curve and was able to work much faster.

Source: Surayut Thavikulwat, Chief Financial Officer, BTS Group Holdings PCL.

Identifying Green Projects, Assets, and Expenditures

The initial step for a bond issuer looking to use the green label for the first time is to identify what they can include in their green bond. The most common approach is to identify hard assets that have green credentials, but there is actually a lot of flexibility in terms of what can be counted as a green project, asset, investment, or expenditure.

A variety of projects, assets, activities, refinancing, new capital, and relevant expenditures are all eligible to be associated with a green bond. The types of projects, assets, and expenditures that can be included in a green bond include (i) owned projects and assets, (ii) financing arrangements for projects and assets, and (iii) related supporting expenditures (Figure 4).

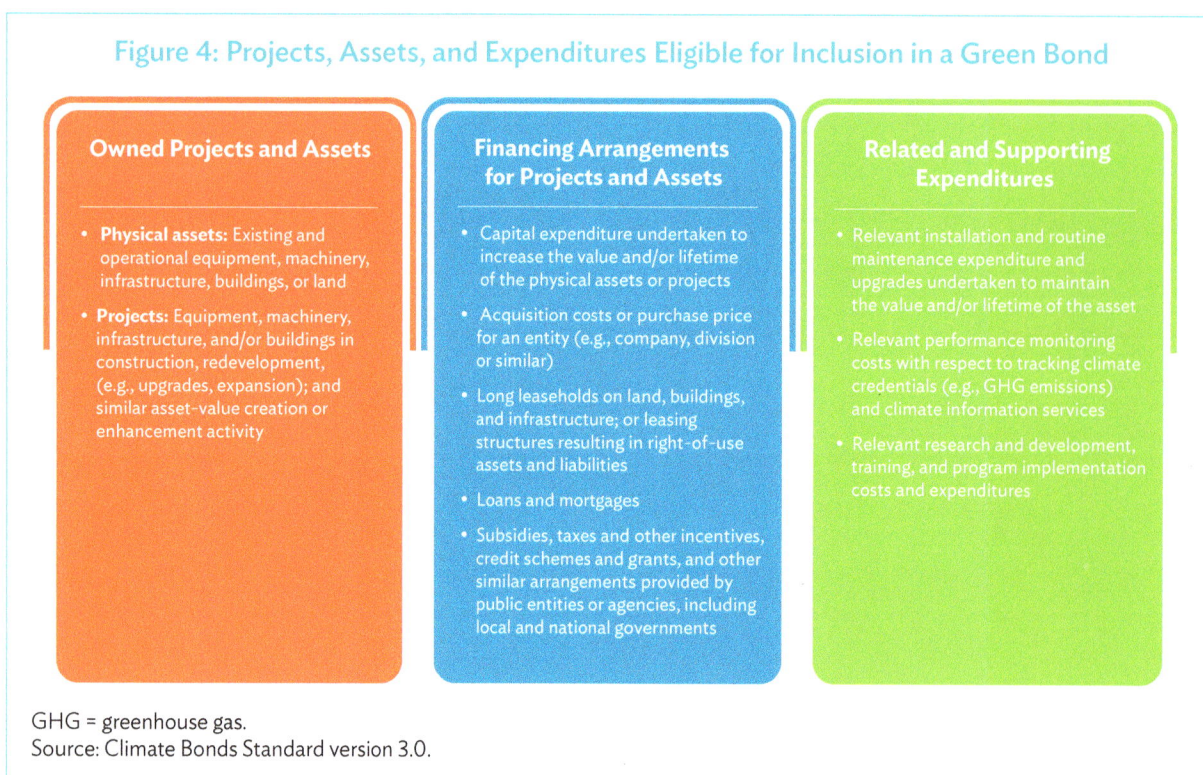

Figure 4: Projects, Assets, and Expenditures Eligible for Inclusion in a Green Bond

Owned Projects and Assets	Financing Arrangements for Projects and Assets	Related and Supporting Expenditures
• **Physical assets:** Existing and operational equipment, machinery, infrastructure, buildings, or land • **Projects:** Equipment, machinery, infrastructure, and/or buildings in construction, redevelopment, (e.g., upgrades, expansion); and similar asset-value creation or enhancement activity	• Capital expenditure undertaken to increase the value and/or lifetime of the physical assets or projects • Acquisition costs or purchase price for an entity (e.g., company, division or similar) • Long leaseholds on land, buildings, and infrastructure; or leasing structures resulting in right-of-use assets and liabilities • Loans and mortgages • Subsidies, taxes and other incentives, credit schemes and grants, and other similar arrangements provided by public entities or agencies, including local and national governments	• Relevant installation and routine maintenance expenditure and upgrades undertaken to maintain the value and/or lifetime of the asset • Relevant performance monitoring costs with respect to tracking climate credentials (e.g., GHG emissions) and climate information services • Relevant research and development, training, and program implementation costs and expenditures

GHG = greenhouse gas.
Source: Climate Bonds Standard version 3.0.

Selecting an Appropriate Set of Green Definitions

Once the underlying projects, assets, and expenditures are identified, green bond issuers need to determine which set of green definitions is going to be used for their selection of green projects and assets. There are a few options available, and it is important to understand the key considerations for this important choice. Many in the green bond market have adopted the word "taxonomy" to describe a set of green definitions (Figure 5).

Figure 5: Green Definitions

CURRENT OPTIONS FOR GREEN DEFINITIONS

GREEN BOND PRINCIPLES HIGH-LEVEL LIST
o   Very broad range of high-level categories for green projects and assets
o   Seen as the minimum level of green ambition
o   Further explanation of green credentials is usually included by issuers

ASEAN GREEN BOND STANDARD
o   Adopted in 2017 and updated in 2018 by the ASEAN Capital Markets Forum
o   Uses high-level list from Green Bond Principles
o   Additional condition that fossil fuel power generation projects must be excluded
o   Issuers must have a geographic or economic connection to ASEAN

NATIONAL OR REGIONAL TAXONOMIES OR GUIDELINES (e.g., Japan, Indonesia, the PRC)
o   The PRC has a **Green Project Catalogue** (updated in 2020).
o   Japan has **Green Bond Guidelines** (updated in 2020).
o   Other ASEAN countries are looking to develop locally relevant taxonomies.

CLIMATE BONDS INITIATIVE TAXONOMY
o   Most commonly used international set of definitions with a focus on climate
o   Used by most green bond index providers and adopted by some external reviewers
o   Also has sector-specific criteria that are used for certification under the Climate Bonds Standard

EUROPEAN UNION'S SUSTAINABLE FINANCE TAXONOMY
o   Very complex approach with additional checks beyond just green credentials
o   Will be expanded beyond climate issues to deal with other sustainability topics
o   May be necessary for green bond issuers to clarify alignment if they are looking to issue their bond in an EU jurisdiction or attract investors from the EU

Legend: ▪ Minimum level   ▪▪▪▪▪ Complex level

KEY CONSIDERATIONS FOR CHOOSING A SET OF GREEN DEFINITIONS

LABELING REQUIREMENTS IN THE JURISDICTION WHERE THE ISSUANCE WILL OCCUR
o   Some jurisdictions require issuers of labeled bonds to follow very specific regulations and approval pathways (e.g., the PRC).
o   Other jurisdictions have voluntary guidelines that add to investor confidence.

MARKETS AND INVESTORS BEING TARGETED FOR THE BOND ISSUANCE
o   If the issuer is targeting local investor, then local definitions are usually enough.
o   For international investors, it may be necessary to use international definitions.

LOCATIONS OF THE GREEN PROJECTS AND ASSETS
o   The relevant jurisdictions may have specific green definitions that need to be used.
o   Definitions used in advanced economies may not be relevant for other markets, especially emerging markets in Asia.

TYPES OF GREEN PROJECTS AND ASSETS AVAILABLE TO THE GREEN BOND ISSUER
o   Green projects and assets can use definitions with more green ambition.
o   Some sectors or subsectors are not covered by existing taxonomies.

INVESTOR AND MARKET PERSPECTIVES ON THE LEVEL OF AMBITION OF GREEN DEFINITIONS
o   Some investors are concerned that definitions with low ambition are riskier from a greenwashing perspective.
o   Most investors are comfortable with the Green Bond Principles' high-level list with extra exclusions for fossil fuel sectors.

ASEAN = Association of Southeast Asian Nations, EU = European Union, PRC = People's Republic of China.
Source: Authors' compilation.

Investors want to see the details of the green projects and assets associated with the bond, but they often do not have the technical background to judge their merits. External reviews of green bonds can provide investors with confidence based on a number of different proprietary approaches and reassuring narratives on green credentials.

Useful links
- Green Bond Principles
- ASEAN Green Bond Standards
- Climate Bonds Taxonomy
- ASEAN Taxonomy for Sustainable Finance
- The PRC's Green Project Catalogue (updated in 2020)
- Japan's Green Bond Guidelines
- European Union's Sustainable Finance Taxonomy
- International Platform on Sustainable Finance's Common Ground Taxonomy

Creating the List

Once the issuer has considered the types of assets, investments, and expenditures that can be used—and selected an appropriate set of green definitions—a list of green projects and assets can be created by the issuer (Figure 6).

Figure 6: Creating the List of Green Projects and Assets

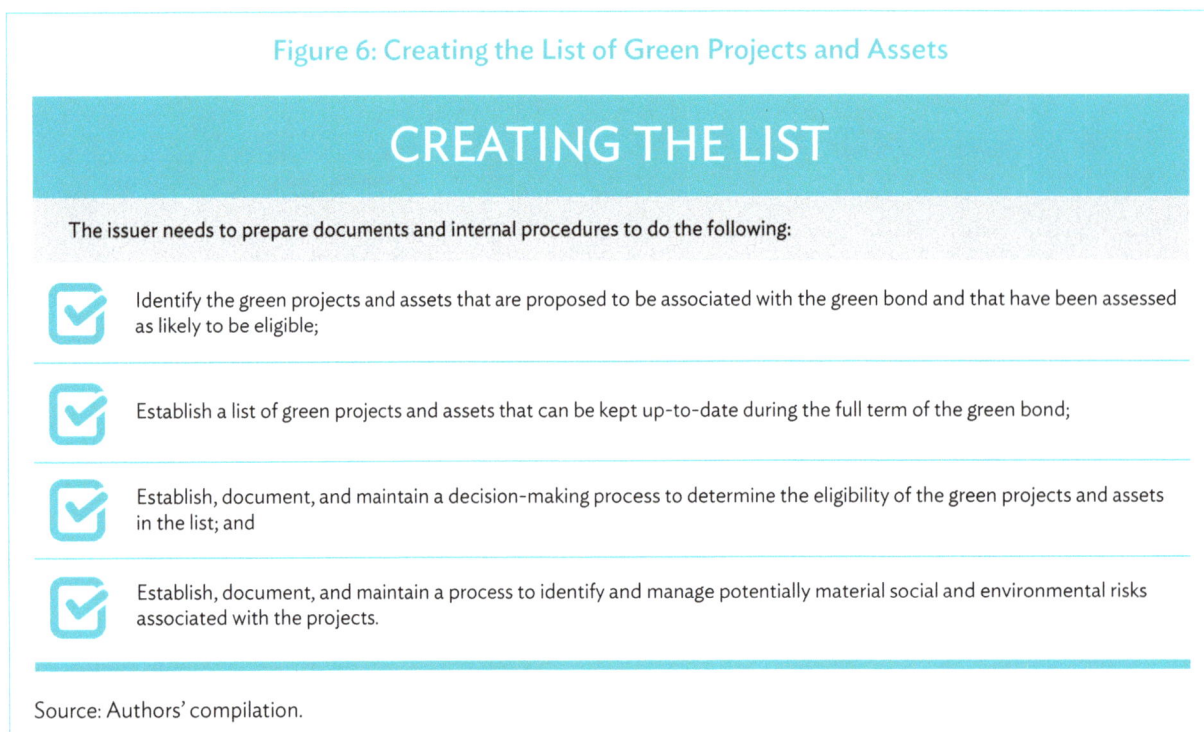

CREATING THE LIST

The issuer needs to prepare documents and internal procedures to do the following:

- ☑ Identify the green projects and assets that are proposed to be associated with the green bond and that have been assessed as likely to be eligible;

- ☑ Establish a list of green projects and assets that can be kept up-to-date during the full term of the green bond;

- ☑ Establish, document, and maintain a decision-making process to determine the eligibility of the green projects and assets in the list; and

- ☑ Establish, document, and maintain a process to identify and manage potentially material social and environmental risks associated with the projects.

Source: Authors' compilation.

These documents and procedures should align with existing processes and governance structures inside the issuer's organization. Many existing structures for decision-making and tracking over time can be used. This will minimize the number of new internal procedures and processes that need to be created by the issuer.

Issuers should seek to clarify any related eligibility and exclusion criteria, as well as any other policies or processes by which the issuer identifies and manages perceived social and environmental risks associated with the selected projects and assets.

The issuer's processes should seek to ensure that the relevant project(s) do not cause significant harm to other environmental and social objectives. The issuer should also communicate its analysis, any mitigation measures enacted, and the monitoring to be undertaken in cases when the issuer assesses the potential risks to be meaningful.

Tracking and Information Flows

Many green projects and assets will be eligible just based on what they are. For example, solar or wind power facilities and electrified transport are all "green enough" based on their role in a future green economy.

Other green projects, assets, and expenditures need to demonstrate their eligibility through performance measures. For example, green commercial buildings or energy efficiency initiatives need to be green enough so that they make a real contribution to achieving a future green economy. Buildings that are slightly cleaner than the average, or small improvements in energy use, are not aligned with what investors want to see in bonds labeled as green.

Sometimes this green performance information is not tracked, or it is not readily available to the green bond issuer. For example, a bank with a loan to a commercial building owner may not receive any green performance information as part of the loan arrangements.

Issuers need to establish processes to track the relevant information for their green projects and assets so that they can demonstrate their green eligibility as well as the relevant impact metrics. This may mean establishing new information flows within the organization or between entities involved with green projects and assets.

Issuers need to ensure that the information flows from relevant sources to the group within the issuing entity that is responsible for reporting are established and working as intended. This is often more complex within a government or public sector structure compared to corporations, but it is equally important for the integrity of the green.

Managing the Green Portfolio Over Time

The use-of-proceeds approach requires specific green projects and assets to be associated with the green bond. However, the green projects and assets identified prior to the issuance of the bond may not be available to the issuer or large enough for the full term of the bond.

Additional green projects, assets, and expenditures can be added to—or used to substitute or replenish—the portfolio of green projects, assets, and expenditures associated with the green bond, as long as the additional projects, assets, and expenditures are eligible under the issuer's green bond framework.

Most issuers of green bonds will regularly update their list of green projects, assets, and expenditures, and then each year disclose the changes in their regular reporting to bond holders.

Issuers of multiple green bonds or other labeled debt instruments can manage their labels on a portfolio basis. This means that multiple green bonds can be "stacked up" and associated with a large pool of green projects and assets. More information on this approach is provided in Further Issuance of Labeled Instruments.

Developing a Green Bond or Sustainable Finance Framework

The issuer of a green bond needs to have a Green Bond Framework, or a Sustainable Finance Framework, that lays out the information required to demonstrate the integrity of the green label. This information is often presented using the four core components of the Green Bond Principles: (i) use of proceeds, (ii) selection of projects and assets, (iii) management of proceeds, and (iv) reporting and external review.

Bond issuers are usually very large organizations, so this framework will often describe how the issuer's existing procedures or governance structures are used as well as any new procedures that have been created for the purpose of a green bond issuance.

Expected Contents

Green bond frameworks can either be quite short (3–5 pages) or very long and detailed (20+ pages). Many examples are available from a wide variety of issuers from over 50 different countries. Figure 7 lists the items that must be included in an issuer's framework document.

Clarity of the Issuer's Narrative

The statements in the objectives of the green bond and the issuer's broader green objectives (Figure 7, items a. and b.) are usually included in the introduction or overview section of the green bond framework.

A wide variety of green objectives are possible. These can vary from increasing the installed capacity of low-carbon assets, such as solar power facilities, to having a specific objective focused on the operations or indirect effects of the projects and assets, such as emissions reductions.

This is a very important aspect of the green bond issuance process because it provides the issuer with the opportunity to directly explain to investors why and how green bonds fit within their long-term vision or corporate strategy.

Many green bonds issuers have already articulated their green or sustainability objectives in corporate sustainability reports or other statements on green topics. Using a green bond to raise money in the capital markets usually complements the issuer's broader green objectives and narrative.

Many green bond investors consider the issuer's profile and take into consideration the quality of the issuer's overall profile and performance regarding environmental sustainability. In the presence of controversial issues—such as fossil fuels, extractive or nuclear-based activities, or limited overall sustainability credentials—investors, stock exchanges, index providers, and other market participants may also require additional transparency from the green bond issuer.

Figure 7: Required Components of a Green Bond Framework

GREEN BOND FRAMEWORK

A	A statement on the green objectives of the green bond;
B	How the green objectives of the green bond are positioned within the context of the issuer's overarching objectives, strategy, policy and/or processes relating to environmental sustainability;
C	Confirmation that the bonds that will be issued under the green bond framework are aligned with one or more established approaches to labeling. This may include statements of alignment with applicable standards such as the Green Bond Principles, the Association of Southeast Asian Nations Green Bond Standards, the Climate Bonds Standard, or local or regional regulations or guidelines;
D	A summary of the green projects and assets that will be associated with the green bond such as sectors covered or geographic distribution;
E	The list of proposed green projects and assets associated with the green bond (if this is available and/or can be disclosed prior to issuance of the green bond);
F	A description of the decision-making process that has been used to select the green projects and assets;
G	A summary of the approach to the management of unallocated proceeds from the green bond and the expected timeline for green bond proceeds to be fully allocated;
H	An estimate of the share of the green bond proceeds that will be used for financing new green projects and assets and the share used for refinancing existing green projects and assets, including the relevant green projects and assets or investment areas that may be refinanced and how long since those green projects and assets were originally financed; and
I	The intended approach to providing update reports while the green bond remains outstanding.

Source: Authors' compilation.

In particular, additional disclosure may be sought around the strategic importance of sustainability for the business, demonstration of the issuer's transition strategy, and/or the sustainability benefits of the underlying projects that go beyond established sector norms and business as usual. It is important that green bond issuers are ready for these discussions.

Flexibility and Updating

A green bond issuer can create a framework that is just for the issuance of one green bond, or they can create a framework for a broader range and number of sustainable finance transactions. Many issuers have created an overarching Green Bond Framework, or a Sustainable Finance Framework, with the potential to issue green bonds, social bonds, green *sukuk*, and sustainability-linked instruments.

Transparency is the most important part of the labeling of bonds and other debt instruments. The Green Bond Framework (or the Sustainable Finance Framework) created by the issuer is the key channel for communicating to investors and other stakeholders the basis and integrity of the label. It is used by external reviewers and index providers, as well as a wide range of market participants.

Updating the framework should occur whenever there is a material change. This can include expanding the range of eligible projects and assets, shifting the focus from green to a broader range of labels, or reflecting a change in the issuer's organization. Most issuers will notify investors and other stakeholders when their framework has been updated, and they often use the opportunity to highlight the progress or ambition of the issuer.

Leveraging Successful Examples

It is very useful to look at other Green Bond Frameworks, and broader Sustainable Finance Frameworks, to understand the level of detail and tone of voice that issuers provide in these documents. There is quite a lot of variety across the many framework documents that have been used for green bond and sustainable finance transactions.

Many examples are available from market information providers or from individual issuer websites. Issuers will benefit from reviewing examples of frameworks that are similar to their own situation. For instance, useful insights can be gained from looking at examples from the same jurisdiction or for similar green projects and assets, organization structures, or targeted investors.

Confirming Internal Processes and Controls

The issuer of a green bond or other labeled debt instrument needs to establish and maintain internal processes and controls. These must enable the issuer to reliably undertake procedures and make decisions on the selection of green projects, assets, expenditures, the management of green bond proceeds, and reporting.

A summary of the issuer's approach needs to be provided in its Green Bond Framework; the issuer also needs to develop internal procedures that guide the actions and decisions of the issuer. The external reviewer will assess the issuer's internal controls and processes as part of the external review process.

Leveraging Existing Arrangements

The actual extent of internal controls and processes for the green bond will depend on the issuer's organization and the existing complexity around information flows and decision-making. For example, a pure-play solar power company is likely to have simple procedures, while a government issuer may have quite complex information flows and decision-making structures to support its green bond or sustainable finance transactions.

Most issuers of green bonds already have comprehensive internal controls and processes for making investment decisions, tracking funds within the business, and signing off on external statements. The key requirements for green bonds can be met by using or adjusting the existing arrangements within the issuer organization.

Creating New Groups and Conversations

While many existing arrangements can be leveraged, the information required for eligibility of the projects, assets, and expenditures may represent new arrangements for sourcing and compiling information as well as requiring new groups to be formed. Many supporters of green bonds have highlighted these new groups and conversations within the issuer as being one of the most valuable outcomes from the effort to use the green label. They provide new channels for discussion and improved understanding of green opportunities and risks across the issuer's organization.

For example, many issuers will set up a green selection committee consisting of senior members of staff from relevant departments (e.g., finance, engineering, and operations). The committee is tasked with screening the underlying projects, assets, and expenditures according to the green definitions and criteria being used. The committee provides recommendations for the selection of projects, assets, and expenditures that is then confirmed (i.e., "signed off") by the issuer's relevant decision-making body or key person.

Similarly, sovereign issuers of green bonds often describe their newly created governance processes for the selection of green projects, assets, and expenditures. For example, relevant projects, assets, and expenditures are screened by a joint committee consisting of representatives of the finance ministry, environment ministry, transport ministry, and other relevant ministries. Selection decisions are then sent to an appropriate body or government ministry for formal approval.

Documentation of Procedures

While each issuer might have a different way of selecting green projects, assets, and expenditures, or of managing the proceeds from the green bond, the key point is that the issuer should be as transparent as possible to provide investors with comfort that the issuer's internal processes and controls are robust.

The internal processes and controls that the issuer uses for its green bond need to be documented. These need to include the following items as detailed in Figure 8.

Figure 8: Key Aspects of the Selection Process for Green Bond Issuance

Selection of green projects and assets

The selection process determines whether the green projects and assets meet the relevant eligibility requirements of the chosen set of green definitions or taxonomy. This should include any green standards or certifications referenced in the selection criteria. It can also refer to exclusion criteria or any other process applied to identify and manage potentially material environmental, social, or governance risks associated with the projects and assets.

Management of the green bond proceeds

These need to cover three key aspects with respect to management of proceeds:

▸ **Tracking of proceeds**
The proceeds of the green bond can be credited to a sub-account, moved to a sub-portfolio (often called "ring-fencing" of proceeds), or otherwise tracked by the issuer in an appropriate manner and documented (often called "earmarking" of proceeds).

▸ **Earmarking funds to green projects and assets**
An earmarking process can be used to manage and account for funding to the green projects and assets and enables estimation of the share of the green bond proceeds being used for financing and refinancing.

▸ **Managing unallocated proceeds**
The balance of the green bond proceeds that have not yet been allocated to green projects and assets can be managed so that the proceeds are not being used for nongreen projects and assets. This usually involves holding cash or cash-equivalent instruments as part of a broader Treasury function.

Reporting on allocations, eligibility, and impact

This refers to processes to bring together all of the relevant information and provide robust reports for internal and external audiences. See further details on reporting in Post-issuance Reporting and Disclosure.

Source: Authors' compilation

Decision-Making, Disclosure, and Governance

Labeling a bond as green (or any other label) requires the issuer to make decisions, disclose to investors and the public, and provide confidence that the label is robust.

Most issuers of green bonds already have these capabilities internally based on their existing business or public sector operations. These should be used as much as possible by the issuer.

Investors and market players want to have confidence that these aspects of the issuer's green bond offering are robust and transparent, even if they are not often interested in the details. External reviewers will assess the issuer's internal processes and controls as part of their review procedures. See Engaging the External Reviewer and Managing the External Review Process for further details.

Reporting on Allocations and Green Credentials

The use-of-proceeds approach is described in the Green Bond Principles' definition of a green bond:[4]

> Any type of bond instrument where the proceeds will be exclusively applied to finance or refinance, in part or in full, new and/or existing eligible green projects, assets, and expenditures that are aligned with the four core components of the Green Bond Principles.

Thus, the value of the green projects, assets, and expenditures must be equal to or higher in value than the amount of the bond to be issued. So if a $100 million green bond is issued, then the issuer needs to have at least $100 million worth of green projects, assets, and expenditures. Most issuers will include a buffer so, for example, they may associate $120 million of green projects, assets, and expenditures with the green bond in this example.

The issuer needs to establish internal mechanisms that allows it to effectively track and allocate proceeds from the labeled bond to eligible projects, assets, and expenditures (Figure 9). These mechanisms are described in the wording of the Green Bond Principles on the topic of management of proceeds (footnote 4):

> The net proceeds of the green bond, or an amount equal to these net proceeds, should be credited to a sub-account, moved to a sub-portfolio, or otherwise tracked by the issuer in an appropriate manner...

Satisfying Green Eligibility Requirements

The eligibility requirements for the issuer's green projects, assets, and expenditures depend on the set of green definitions, or taxonomy, that the issuer is using. The choice of taxonomy has a major impact on whether projects, assets, and expenditures will be "green enough" to be associated with a green bond.

Some of the taxonomies are very prescriptive in what is needed to demonstrate eligibility, but this also depends on the types of projects, assets, and expenditures being considered. For example, for assets such as solar farms, wind farms, or electrified public transport, green eligibility is based on the core properties of the assets themselves. No further evidence is required beyond their existence and the value ascribed to them in the issuer's list.

For other assets such as green buildings or hydropower facilities, there is a much broader range of eligibility requirements contained in the various taxonomies. This means that investors will often require more detailed

4   International Capital Market Association. Green Bond Principles. https://www.icmagroup.org/sustainable-finance/the-principles-guidelines-and-handbooks/green-bond-principles-gbp/.

Figure 9: Two Approaches to the Allocation of Proceeds

Ringfencing. This occurs when the issuer decides to separate the proceeds from its business-as-usual operations by putting the proceeds into a specific sub-account or sub-portfolio. For instance, ringfencing could happen when a portfolio of solar farms is being financed and the proceeds are held in a special purpose vehicle for each of the wind farms.

Earmarking. The proceeds enter the balance sheet of the issuer and are matched up, or "allocated," to the issuer's list of green projects and assets so that the proceeds are "tracked by the issuer in an appropriate manner." There is no segregation of proceeds in separate sub-accounts. This is common practice among issuers of green bonds (including sovereign issuers) and is widely used to finance future capital investment or to refinance investments in longer-term projects.

Source: Authors' compilation.

information about projects, assets, and expenditures in these categories, which flows through to the issuer needing to obtain and provide that information. This could include certifications for green buildings or actual performance data if that is the form of an eligibility threshold.

For green definitions that only apply to the Green Bond Principles high-level categories, there is much more flexibility for the issuer to define its own green eligibility requirements. Issuers need to ensure that they are transparent on the eligibility of the green projects, assets, and expenditures associated with their green bonds. This may include demonstrating the eligibility of existing projects, assets, and expenditures, or defining criteria for new projects, assets, and expenditures (Figure 10).

Figure 10: Examples of Green Definitions

Example 1. Commercial buildings under Climate Bonds Taxonomy are defined as being in the top 15% of the buildings in that city in terms of greenhouse gas performance per square meter of net lettable area. The Green Bond Principles' high-level categories have no thresholds for green buildings, so the issuer can choose any approach to eligibility, such as "better than building code" or "20% better than average."

Example 2. Hydropower is a source of renewable energy, but is also controversial for many investors based on the social and environmental impacts of hydropower development. Under the ASEAN Green Bond Standard, all renewable energy is eligible; while under the Climate Bonds Standard, there are substantial requirements for hydropower assets. Furthermore, under the Climate Bonds Standard, any hydropower asset must meet a threshold based on its greenhouse gas emissions footprint as well as undergo a site-specific assessment using the Environmental, Social, and Governance Gap Analysis Tool.

ASEAN = Association of Southeast Asian Nations.
Source: Authors' compilation.

Investor and Market Expectations

Prior to issuance of the green bond, the issuer's Green Bond Framework plays an important role in providing transparency for potential investors on
- what green projects, assets, and expenditures will be associated with the green bond;
- whether the selected projects, assets, and expenditures are green enough; and
- how the issuer will report on these things during the term of the green bond.

After the green bond has been issued, the issuer is expected to prepare an update report at least annually, while the green bond remains outstanding, and on a timely basis if there are any material developments in the bond's green label. The update report includes information on the allocation of proceeds; eligibility of green projects, assets, and expenditures; and impact reporting. See Post-Issuance Reporting and Disclosure for further details.

Material developments could include early repayment of the bond; change of control or acquisition; change of name; changes to the eligibility of assets or projects; as well as any material amendments, supplements, and other updates to deal documents.

The issuer needs to make the update report available to holders of the green bond and is strongly encouraged to make the report available to the public. If the update report cannot be made available to the public, then the green bond may not be aligned with some of the more stringent approaches to identifying green bonds that require public disclosure of annual reports.

Reporting Formats and Channels

Green bond issuers provide their information in a wide variety of formats. Sometimes, the information is included in a broader sustainability report for the organization. Often, the green bond report is provided by the issuer as a separate document.

For new issuers of green bonds, it is good to look at examples of what other issuers have done to understand the level of detail and tone of voice in similar circumstances.

Most green bond issuers provide their green bond documents on a "sustainability" or "green bonds" page on their website. This enables investors to easily access the information on a regular basis. The timing of providing the update report can be aligned with the issuer's schedule of regular reporting and does not need to follow the anniversary of the issuance of the green bond.

Other channels include various market information providers such as *AsianBondsOnline*, Environmental Finance, the Climate Bonds Initiative (CBI), and stock exchanges.

Issuers are encouraged to make the update reports available through existing reporting channels for the capital markets, such as the issuer's website, a stock exchange information dissemination portal, or a local green bond platform. This streamlines the information-gathering process for investors and analysts, further strengthening the value of the green label and reducing transaction costs.

Setting Up for Impact Reporting

Green projects, assets, and expenditures have a wide variety of environmental impacts. This is not surprising given the diverse range of green sectors, subsectors, and supporting infrastructure that have already been supported by green bonds.

There is much focus on impact reporting by green bond investors. This is often the focus of asset managers who buy green bonds in the market and then sell their green investment products to investors. They want to have quantified green impacts from each of the green bonds to assist with demonstrating the green credentials of their funds or products.

However, the impacts recognized by green bond investors are actually indicators that cover the outputs, outcomes, and impacts from green projects, assets, and expenditures. Therefore, the focus for green bond issuers should be on impact indicators that can be readily derived from the information they already have available to them.

Input–Output–Outcome–Impact Frameworks

Many projects are designed and evaluated based on a framework that covers the progression from inputs and activities through to impacts. Figure 11 illustrates this framework.

Based on the framework in Figure 11, impact reporting in the green bond market could perhaps be better described as indicator reporting, where the indicators reported by green bond issuers include a variety of outputs, outcomes, and impacts.

Key indicators for specific green sectors, subsectors, and supporting infrastructure have been suggested and compiled by a working group under the Green Bond Principles. The group has published and continues to update the handbook, *Harmonized Framework for Impact Reporting*, which provides useful suggestions for indicators from a growing list of sectors.

Examples of Impact Indicators

The flow from outputs, such as renewable energy capacity installed, through to impacts, such as greenhouse gas (GHG) emissions avoided, can often require many assumptions and detailed methodologies (Figure 12).

For example, in the case of a wind farm, the output is the installed capacity. The outcome is the production of electricity with zero GHG emissions. The impact is GHG emissions avoided, based on the potential displacement of fossil fuel electricity sources from the same grid compared to what would have happened if the wind farm were not operating.

Figure 11: Input–Output–Outcome–Impact Frameworks

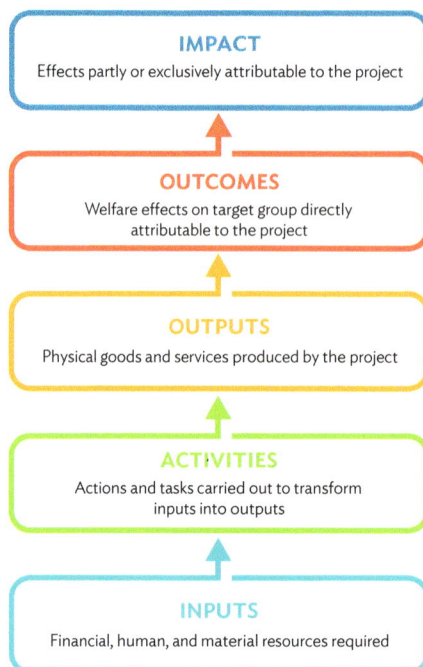

IMPACT
Effects partly or exclusively attributable to the project

OUTCOMES
Welfare effects on target group directly attributable to the project

OUTPUTS
Physical goods and services produced by the project

ACTIVITIES
Actions and tasks carried out to transform inputs into outputs

INPUTS
Financial, human, and material resources required

Source: Authors' compilation.

Figure 12: Examples of Impact Indicators

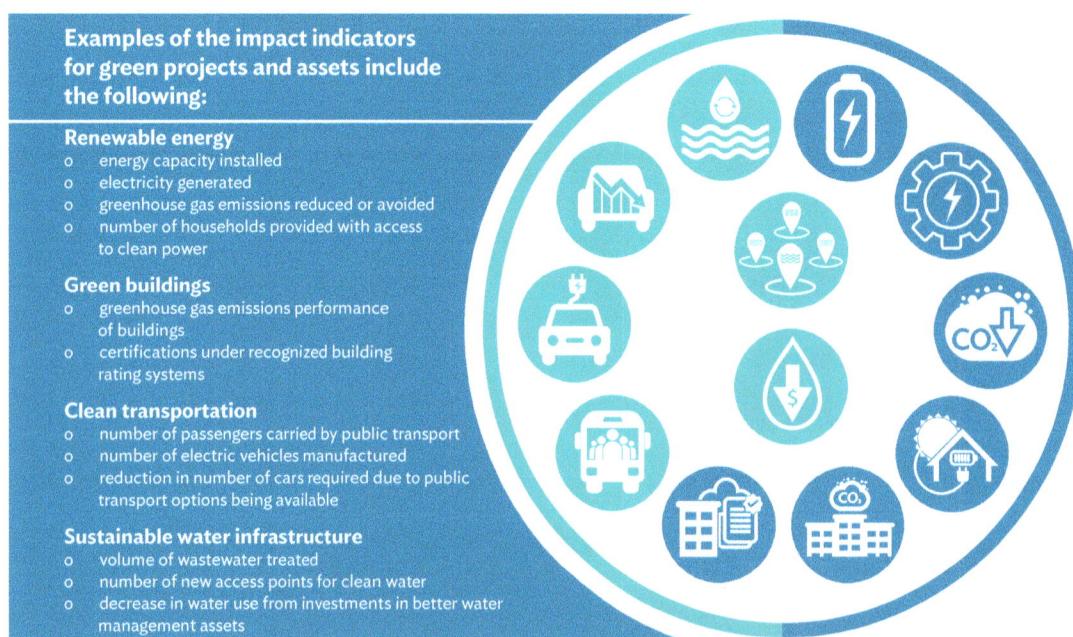

Examples of the impact indicators for green projects and assets include the following:

Renewable energy
o   energy capacity installed
o   electricity generated
o   greenhouse gas emissions reduced or avoided
o   number of households provided with access to clean power

Green buildings
o   greenhouse gas emissions performance of buildings
o   certifications under recognized building rating systems

Clean transportation
o   number of passengers carried by public transport
o   number of electric vehicles manufactured
o   reduction in number of cars required due to public transport options being available

Sustainable water infrastructure
o   volume of wastewater treated
o   number of new access points for clean water
o   decrease in water use from investments in better water management assets

Source: Authors' compilation.

The methods used by the issuer for measuring or estimating the impacts of green projects, assets, and expenditures need to be disclosed in the impact report. Methods include the framework used and the calculation methodology, including if metrics are annual, annualized, and/or lifetime calculations.

Both proprietary and institutional frameworks may be used, institutional frameworks may be referenced, and proprietary and new frameworks should be described in sufficient detail to allow assessment. Examples of institutional and proprietary frameworks are the *Harmonized Framework for Impact Reporting* (institutional) and the *Nordic Public Sector Issuers: Position Paper on Green Bond Impact Reporting* (proprietary).

Ex Post versus Ex Ante Reporting

The expected impacts from green projects, assets, and expenditures (known as ex ante) are usually estimated as part of the formulation of the green bond, and the estimates are often reported as part of the pre-issuance disclosure from a green bond issuer.

Gathering ex post information on the actual performance and impacts of green projects, assets, and expenditures can create a substantial workload for issuers. This is a key consideration for green bond issuers, especially if their portfolio of green projects, assets, and expenditures cover a variety of green sectors.

There is usually a lot of effort, cost, and potential risk involved with the issuer providing ex post information in reports, but this is greatly applauded by investors.

The use of ex ante information (estimates of impact) can be easier for issuers, and it is usually enough to satisfy investors when looking for relevant impact indicators.

The Green Bond Principles recommend the use of qualitative indicators and, where feasible, quantitative performance measures of expected impact. Issuers with the ability to report achieved impacts are encouraged to include those also in their regular update reporting.

Data and Systems

More and more companies and public organizations are using purpose-built systems to capture relevant green and sustainability data and produce the information they need for reporting. These systems make it easier for external reviewers to verify information flows and data integrity, as well as provide up-to-date information for management reporting.

Green bond issuers with large portfolios of green projects, assets, and expenditures are encouraged to adopt these systems to ensure the integrity of their green portfolios over time and simplify their regular processes for compiling and confirming reports. This is particularly important for dynamic green portfolios, where projects, assets, and expenditures are entering and leaving the green list in between the annual allocation reports being provided.

Engaging the External Reviewer

All of the principles and guidelines for labeling a green bond include strong recommendations that issuers engage an external reviewer to provide an opinion on the green label. In many jurisdictions, it is mandatory for green labels to be accompanied by an opinion from an external reviewer.

The most comprehensive list of external reviewers is provided by the CBI, which has an approved verifier program to ensure the quality of the service providers. There is also a list available from the Green Bond Principles website.

Scoping Out What You Need

There are four different external review products that are used in the green bond market (Figure 13). The most common approach is a second-party opinion (or "second opinion"), while there is increasing use of certification approaches that rely on national, regional, or international standards or guidelines. Most external reviewer providers will offer multiple types of external review so it is up to the issuer to choose which is the most appropriate for their situation.

The type of external review selected by the green bond issuer will depend on a few key considerations:
- **Jurisdiction of issuance.** Are there regulations or guidelines that specify what type of external review must be used?
- **Investor preference.** Some investors have very strong preferences for the type of external review that should be undertaken. Do the target investors have these preferences?
- **Best practice narrative.** Is the issuer claiming they are using best practice in formulating their green bond? If so, then certification or a strong second-party opinion are more aligned with those claims.

Engagement Contracts

The external reviewer is traditionally engaged (contracted) by the green bond issuer, although this is not always the case. Sometimes, a different entity involved in the green bond transaction may have an easier pathway to engaging a service provider.

For example, in the municipal bond market in the United States, the issuer is restricted by regulations on what can be included in the transaction costs for the bond issuance. In this case, the arranging bank or securities firm supporting the issuance can engage the external reviewer.

Figure 13: The Four Types of External Review

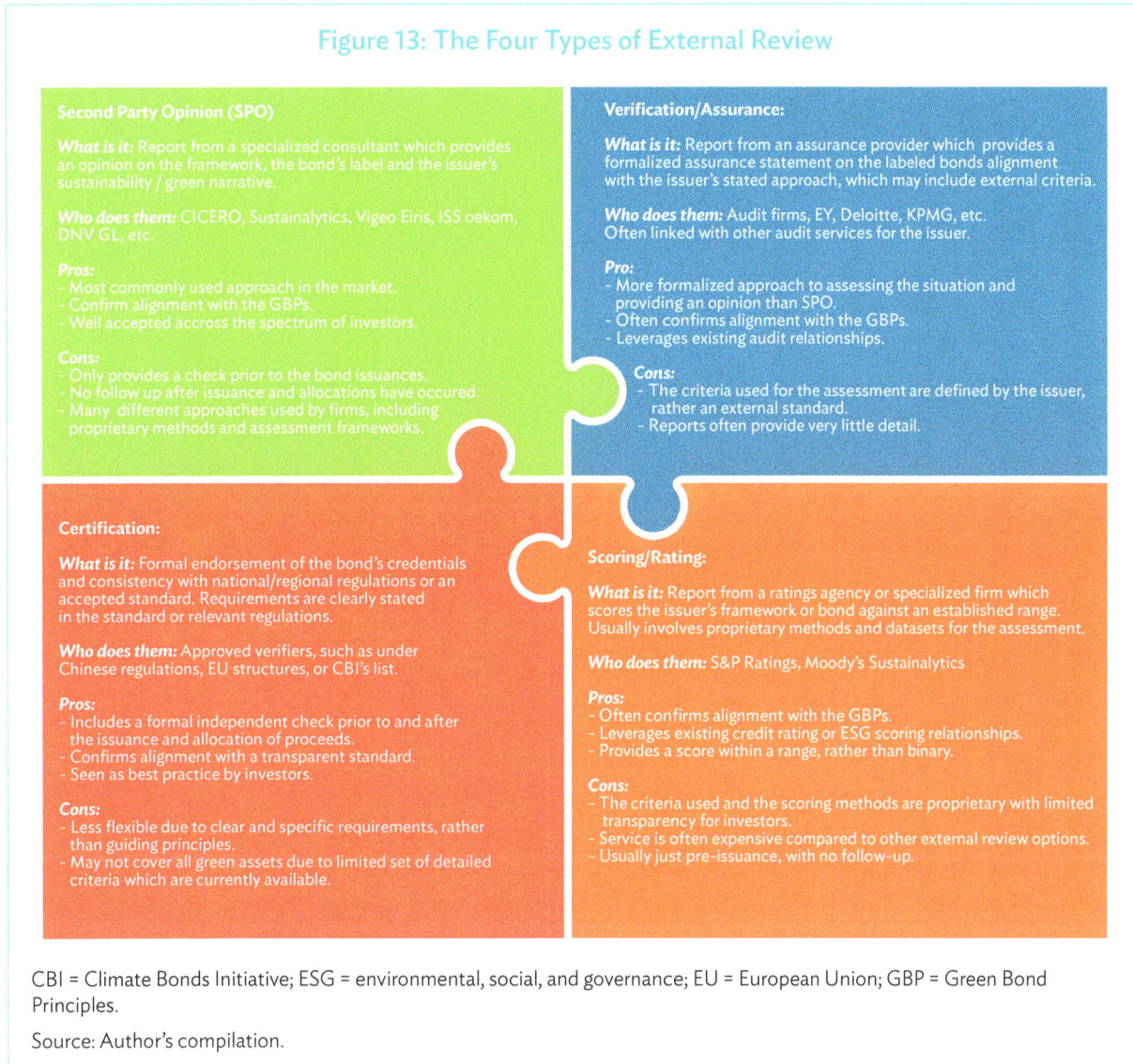

Second Party Opinion (SPO)

What is it: Report from a specialized consultant which provides an opinion on the framework, the bond's label and the issuer's sustainability / green narrative.

Who does them: CICERO, Sustainalytics, Vigeo Eiris, ISS oekom, DNV GL, etc.

Pros:
- Most commonly used approach in the market.
- Confirm alignment with the GBPs.
- Well accepted accross the spectrum of investors.

Cons:
- Only provides a check prior to the bond issuances.
- No follow up after issuance and allocations have occured.
- Many different approaches used by firms, including proprietary methods and assessment frameworks.

Verification/Assurance:

What is it: Report from an assurance provider which provides a formalized assurance statement on the labeled bonds alignment with the issuer's stated approach, which may include external criteria.

Who does them: Audit firms, EY, Deloitte, KPMG, etc. Often linked with other audit services for the issuer.

Pro:
- More formalized approach to assessing the situation and providing an opinion than SPO.
- Often confirms alignment with the GBPs.
- Leverages existing audit relationships.

Cons:
- The criteria used for the assessment are defined by the issuer, rather an external standard.
- Reports often provide very little detail.

Certification:

What is it: Formal endorsement of the bond's credentials and consistency with national/regional regulations or an accepted standard. Requirements are clearly stated in the standard or relevant regulations.

Who does them: Approved verifiers, such as under Chinese regulations, EU structures, or CBI's list.

Pros:
- Includes a formal independent check prior to and after the issuance and allocation of proceeds.
- Confirms alignment with a transparent standard.
- Seen as best practice by investors.

Cons:
- Less flexible due to clear and specific requirements, rather than guiding principles.
- May not cover all green assets due to limited set of detailed criteria which are currently available.

Scoring/Rating:

What is it: Report from a ratings agency or specialized firm which scores the issuer's framework or bond against an established range. Usually involves proprietary methods and datasets for the assessment.

Who does them: S&P Ratings, Moody's Sustainalytics

Pros:
- Often confirms alignment with the GBPs.
- Leverages existing credit rating or ESG scoring relationships.
- Provides a score within a range, rather than binary.

Cons:
- The criteria used and the scoring methods are proprietary with limited transparency for investors.
- Service is often expensive compared to other external review options.
- Usually just pre-issuance, with no follow-up.

CBI = Climate Bonds Initiative; ESG = environmental, social, and governance; EU = European Union; GBP = Green Bond Principles.

Source: Author's compilation.

The contract with the external reviewer should specify the following:
- scope of the work;
- form of the opinion being provided, including any formal alignment or conformance with the Green Bond Principles, ASEAN Green Bond Standards, or Climate Bond Standard;
- expected timeline for the work;
- approach being used by the external reviewer to formulate its opinion, including any standards or other professional services codes of conduct;
- obligations of each party to provide information and undertake the assessment; and
- expected use of the external reviewer's report.

Best practice is to have a single engagement contract that covers the pre-issuance activities as well as the post-issuance assessment.

The external reviewer will often ask to see draft versions of the issuer's key documents before they can determine their level of effort and, hence, the price for the engagement.

Pre-Issuance and Post-Issuance Assessments

Best practice entails having an external review prior to the issuance of the green bond and at least one external review after the green bond has been issued.

Pre-Issuance external review involves the assessment and confirmation of the bond issuer's green bond framework and internal processes, including the:
- selection process for projects and assets,
- systems for internal tracking of proceeds,
- allocation system for funds, and
- reporting arrangements.

This results in an external reviewer's report that can be provided to potential investors and other stakeholders prior to the issuance of the green bond.

A public version of the external reviewer's report is often disclosed to the public after the bond has been issued, usually via the issuer's website. This disclosure of the external reviewer's report is also a key requirement for many market information and index providers.

Post-Issuance external review involves the assessment and confirmation of the green bond's label, which must be undertaken after the allocation of bond proceeds is underway.

The external reviewer undertakes procedures so that it can provide confirmation that the issuer and the bond actually meets all of the nominated requirements (e.g., Green Bond Principles, ASEAN Green Bond Standards, or Climate Bonds Standard, among others).

The post-issuance external review process is focused on
- confirming that the green bond that has been issued is in line with the green bond framework provided prior to issuance;
- confirming that the internal processes examined during the pre-issuance external review are working as expected;
- examining the allocations of net proceeds that have been made so far and the information provided on eligibility (and impacts) for those projects and assets; and
- assessing any update reports that have been provided by the issuer, or the internal processes to generate those reports.

The external reviewer provides a finalized report to the issuer, who then provides the report to the bond holders and other stakeholders, such as regulators or certification systems, as part of their regular reporting and disclosure on the green bond.

Pricing and Timing Expectations

Most green bond issuers describe the costs of the external reviewer as low compared to the other transaction costs associated with issuing a bond such as credit ratings, legal support, investor road shows, and lead manager fees.

However, the timeline for external review is a major consideration for the issuer's approach to raising capital via a bond issuance. Some lead time needs to be built into the issuer's timeline for going to market with the bond offering. Six weeks is a common time frame for an external review to go from contracting to delivery of the final report.

Figure 14 shows the three key considerations that determine the timing and costs of the external review for a green bond label.

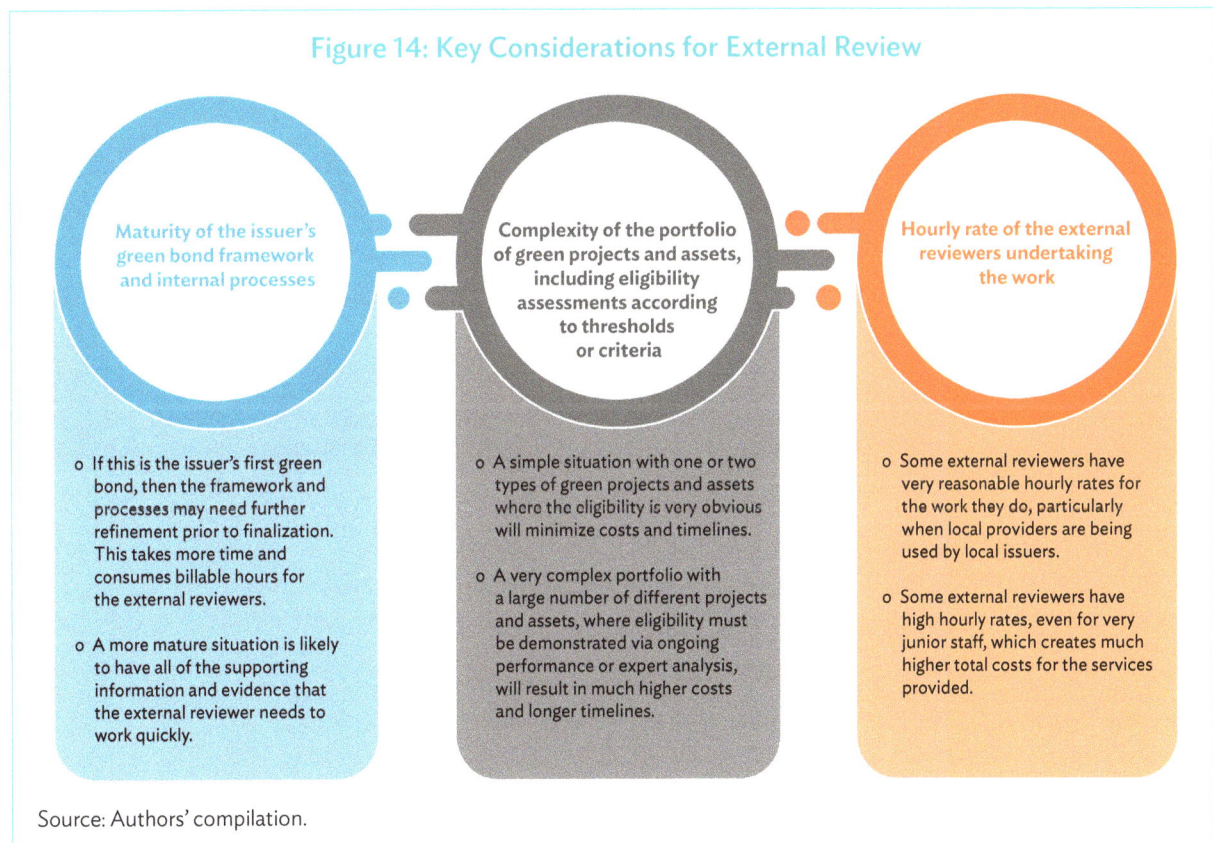

Figure 14: Key Considerations for External Review

Maturity of the issuer's green bond framework and internal processes

o If this is the issuer's first green bond, then the framework and processes may need further refinement prior to finalization. This takes more time and consumes billable hours for the external reviewers.

o A more mature situation is likely to have all of the supporting information and evidence that the external reviewer needs to work quickly.

Complexity of the portfolio of green projects and assets, including eligibility assessments according to thresholds or criteria

o A simple situation with one or two types of green projects and assets where the eligibility is very obvious will minimize costs and timelines.

o A very complex portfolio with a large number of different projects and assets, where eligibility must be demonstrated via ongoing performance or expert analysis, will result in much higher costs and longer timelines.

Hourly rate of the external reviewers undertaking the work

o Some external reviewers have very reasonable hourly rates for the work they do, particularly when local providers are being used by local issuers.

o Some external reviewers have high hourly rates, even for very junior staff, which creates much higher total costs for the services provided.

Source: Authors' compilation.

Many jurisdictions are offering support to issuers who engage external reviewers. This comes in the form of capped subsidies or other contributions, and are currently in place in a number of ASEAN+3 markets.

Managing the External Review Process

The early years of the green bond market saw a lot of issuers use "self-labeling." This was accepted by many investors because at that time all green bond issuers were either multilateral development banks or other very trusted entities.

As the diversity of green bond issuers grew, investors wanted to have more confidence that the green claims being made by the issuer were valid. The investors also recognized the value of having an expert provide an opinion when the investor's own green understanding was limited.

In today's green bond market, there are still a few entities who use self-labeling, but this number is shrinking. The vast majority of green bonds have an external review prior to issuance. A smaller number of issuers have an external review after the issuance, but this trend is increasing.

External reviewers are essentially providing an audit function, but the focus is not like we see in financial auditing.

Sharing Information with the External Reviewer

The external reviewer needs the issuer to provide relevant information. Often the external reviewer will have template information requests that it uses at various stages of the process.

This first occurs during the engagement process, where the external reviewer needs to understand the issuer's situation and green bond plans so that they can prepare a quote and expected timeline for the engagement contract. Usually, it involves the issuer providing a draft green bond framework document and some supporting information.

During the external review, the issuer will then need to provide a more formalized package of information to support the statements in its green bond framework and to demonstrate green eligibility.

External Review Procedures

External reviewers use a variety of procedures to understand the situation and arrive at an opinion. The actual procedures used range from formal information requests to telephone interviews, use of external data sources, site visits, and clarification requests.

Generally, the pre-issuance external review process follows the eight steps outlined in Figure 15.

Figure 15: Pre-Issuance External Review Process

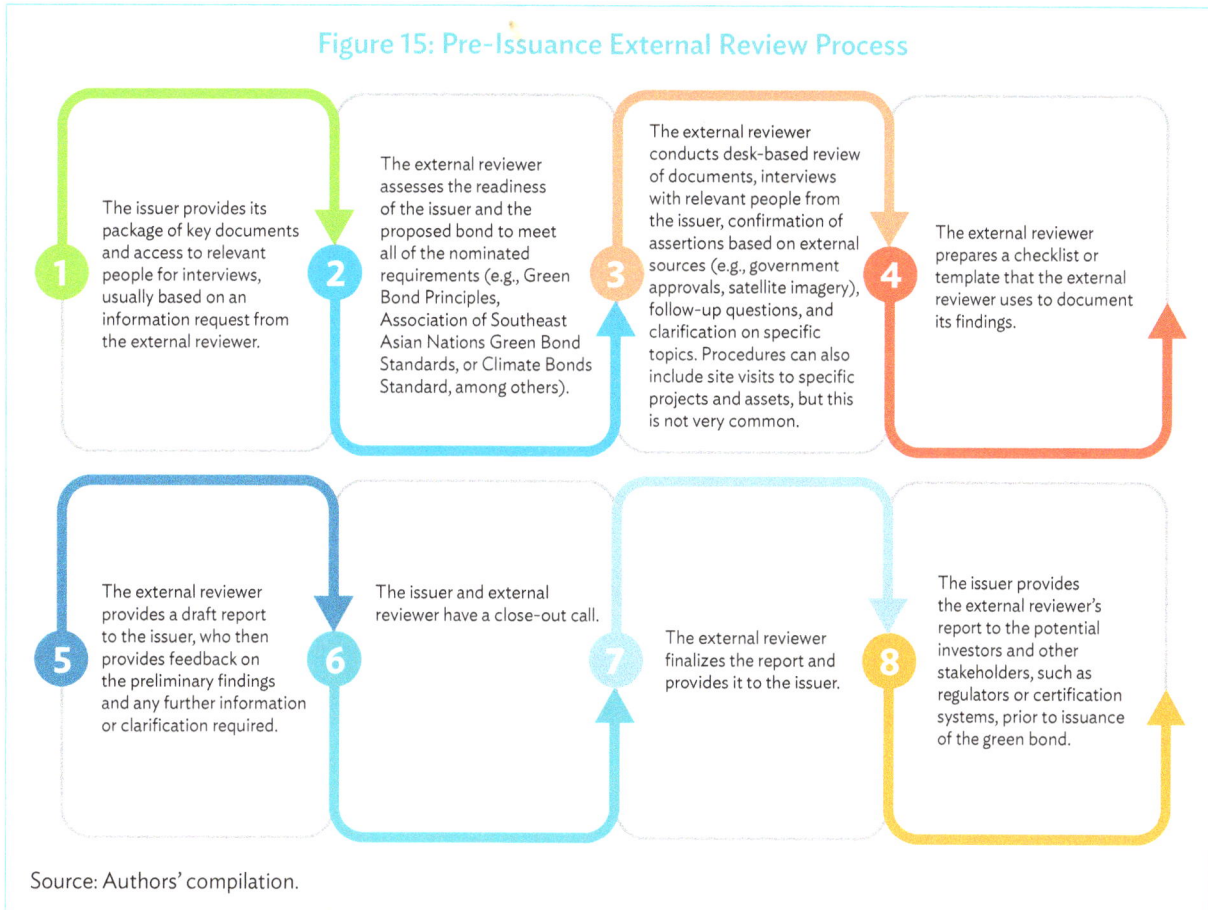

1 The issuer provides its package of key documents and access to relevant people for interviews, usually based on an information request from the external reviewer.	**2** The external reviewer assesses the readiness of the issuer and the proposed bond to meet all of the nominated requirements (e.g., Green Bond Principles, Association of Southeast Asian Nations Green Bond Standards, or Climate Bonds Standard, among others).	**3** The external reviewer conducts desk-based review of documents, interviews with relevant people from the issuer, confirmation of assertions based on external sources (e.g., government approvals, satellite imagery), follow-up questions, and clarification on specific topics. Procedures can also include site visits to specific projects and assets, but this is not very common.	**4** The external reviewer prepares a checklist or template that the external reviewer uses to document its findings.
5 The external reviewer provides a draft report to the issuer, who then provides feedback on the preliminary findings and any further information or clarification required.	**6** The issuer and external reviewer have a close-out call.	**7** The external reviewer finalizes the report and provides it to the issuer.	**8** The issuer provides the external reviewer's report to the potential investors and other stakeholders, such as regulators or certification systems, prior to issuance of the green bond.

Source: Authors' compilation.

Draft Reports and Close-Out Processes

The external reviewer will provide a draft report when they have completed the main body of assessment work. The draft report will highlight any gaps that still need to be filled and provide a preliminary opinion. The issuer needs to respond to the report, clarify any remaining topics, and then confirm that they want the report finalized, usually in a close-out meeting with the external reviewer.

The external reviewer will often have internal processes and quality control that will be part of moving from the draft report to the final opinion and report.

Form and Use of Final Reports

The report from the external reviewer is seen as a key component of any green bond offering, along with the issuer's green bond framework document.

Often the draft report provided to the issuer will have much more detail than a cut-down report that can be used by the issuer for its green bond marketing and then be published after the issuance of the bond.

The final report and opinion are sometimes very brief (e.g., a few pages) even though there has been a lot of work completed to reach that final opinion.

Seeking Certification or Recognition

The process of issuing a green bond can help the financing function of the issuing organization and enable senior management to think more actively about how sustainability relates to their business and operations.

Issuers have access to new investors and a wider range of investors if they can label their bond as green. Deeper investor engagement is also a key benefit for green bond issuers, creating more enduring investor relationships.

For many issuers, there is a benefit in terms of pricing for their green bond compared to other bonds that are not labeled. This price differential, which is often called a "greenium," is usually driven by the large demand for green bonds compared to the emerging supply.

Investor and Market Expectations

As green bond markets have grown and attracted increased attention, there is more mainstreaming of investors who buy into these instruments. While a certain group of investors are those with green mandates and ESG investing activities, there is also increased uptake by so-called "vanilla investors."

Large pension funds and asset managers are increasingly looking for sustainability and low-carbon investments; often, these green bonds are exactly what they are looking for.

Box 2: Experience of Public Debt Management Office, Ministry of Finance, Thailand

Patricia Mongkhonvanit, Director-General, Public Debt Management Office announced that on the 13 August 2020, book building was held for the Kingdom of Thailand's inaugural sustainability bond issuance, which is first of its kind in ASEAN.

The groundbreaking transaction was highly successful with exceptionally strong demand from the investors with amount submitted totaling THB60,911 million, 3.05 times the announced offering, and attracting an interest rate of 1.585%, which is lower than the market yield of the existing 15-year benchmark bond.

Moreover, the sustainability bond attracted a diversified group of investors including banks, asset management companies, financial institutions, insurance companies, and offshore investors.

Source: Government of Thailand, Public Debt Management Office.

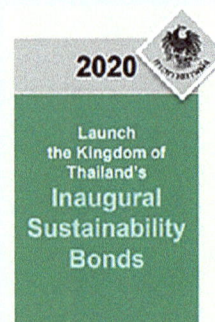

2020
Launch the Kingdom of Thailand's **Inaugural Sustainability Bonds**

There are substantial climate change risks to insurers, and they are becoming increasingly aware of this long-term challenge. Raising the amount of low-carbon investments in their portfolio is part of that long-term risk mitigation.

Investors, stock exchanges, index providers, and other market participants also consider green bonds against their own environmental assessment standards and investment criteria that may set target thresholds for energy efficiency improvements and include broader ESG requirements.

Some of these market participants and stakeholders exclude bonds funding fossil fuel-related projects, while others may, for instance, include energy efficiency investments that do not facilitate a long-term lock-in of high-carbon infrastructure.

International versus Regional versus National Approaches

There are different approaches to gaining recognition or certification of a green bond. This situation is evolving quickly as the market grows and covers a wider variety of sectors and jurisdictions.

More and more regional and national approaches are being defined by governments and regulators. This is a sign that many see great potential in green bonds as a way to drive improved climate outcomes in their own jurisdictions as well as on the international stage (Figure 16).

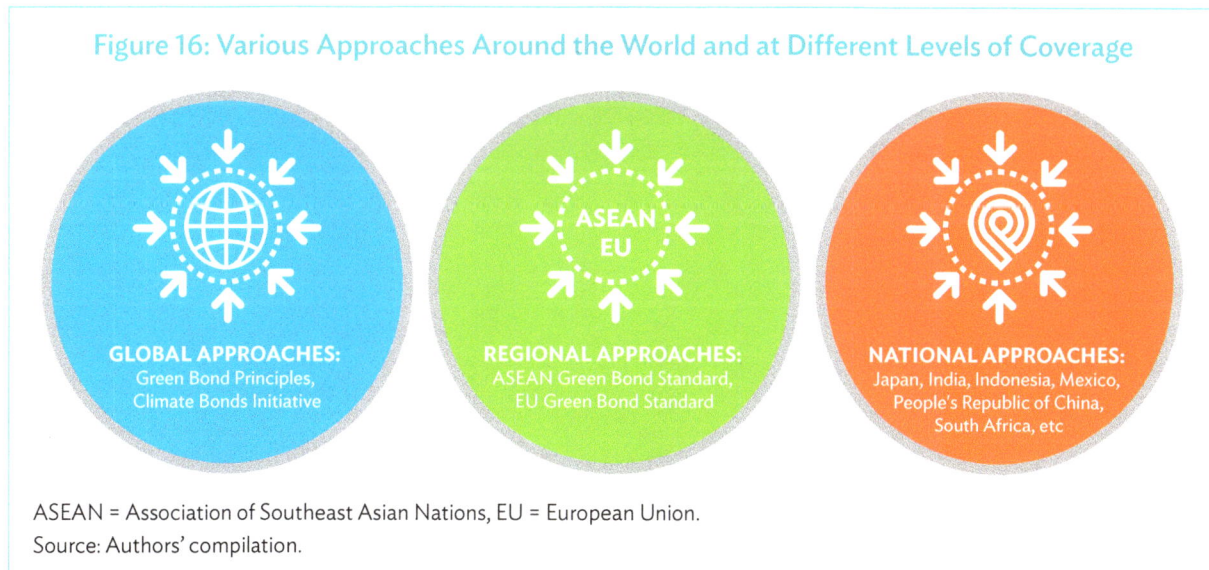

Figure 16: Various Approaches Around the World and at Different Levels of Coverage

GLOBAL APPROACHES:
Green Bond Principles,
Climate Bonds Initiative

REGIONAL APPROACHES:
ASEAN Green Bond Standard,
EU Green Bond Standard

ASEAN
EU

NATIONAL APPROACHES:
Japan, India, Indonesia, Mexico,
People's Republic of China,
South Africa, etc

ASEAN = Association of Southeast Asian Nations, EU = European Union.
Source: Authors' compilation.

International best practices, such as certification under the Climate Bonds Standard, will always be well received by investors and market commentators. However, demand for green bonds is so strong that less stringent approaches, such as alignment with the Green Bond Principles, will be sufficient for most potential investors.

Pathways for Recognition

There are a number of different pathways for recognition for a green bond label (Figure 17). Each of them has specific requirements, but all of them are based on the platform provided by the Green Bond Principles.

The recognition of the green label can come in different forms:
- alignment with Green Bond Principles,
- conformance with the ASEAN Green Bond Standards,
- certification under the Climate Bonds Standard, or
- alignment with specific national guidelines or listing requirements.

Figure 17: Case Studies for Selecting Pathways for Recognition

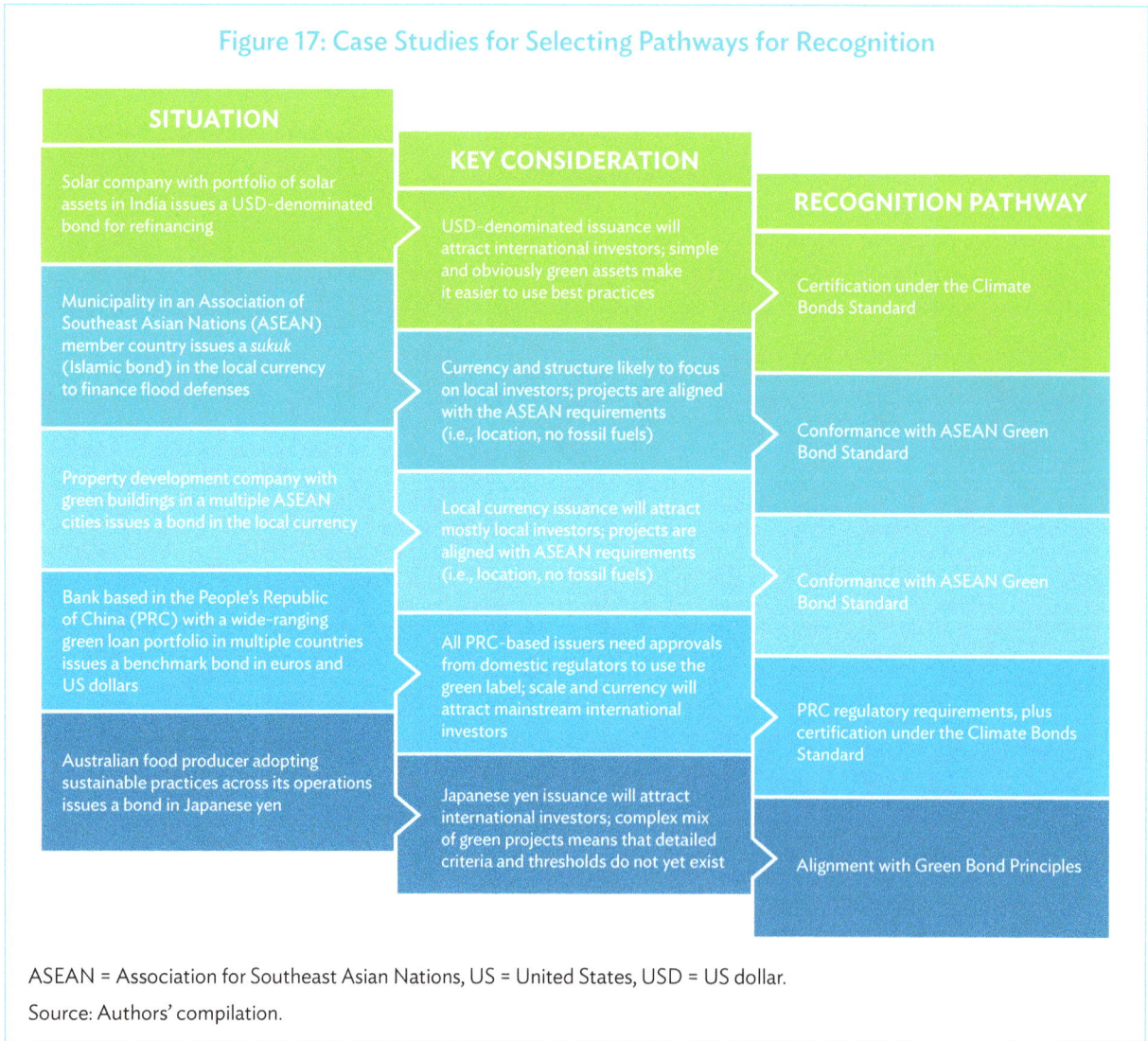

SITUATION	KEY CONSIDERATION	RECOGNITION PATHWAY
Solar company with portfolio of solar assets in India issues a USD-denominated bond for refinancing	USD-denominated issuance will attract international investors; simple and obviously green assets make it easier to use best practices	Certification under the Climate Bonds Standard
Municipality in an Association of Southeast Asian Nations (ASEAN) member country issues a *sukuk* (Islamic bond) in the local currency to finance flood defenses	Currency and structure likely to focus on local investors; projects are aligned with the ASEAN requirements (i.e., location, no fossil fuels)	Conformance with ASEAN Green Bond Standard
Property development company with green buildings in a multiple ASEAN cities issues a bond in the local currency	Local currency issuance will attract mostly local investors; projects are aligned with ASEAN requirements (i.e., location, no fossil fuels)	Conformance with ASEAN Green Bond Standard
Bank based in the People's Republic of China (PRC) with a wide-ranging green loan portfolio in multiple countries issues a benchmark bond in euros and US dollars	All PRC-based issuers need approvals from domestic regulators to use the green label; scale and currency will attract mainstream international investors	PRC regulatory requirements, plus certification under the Climate Bonds Standard
Australian food producer adopting sustainable practices across its operations issues a bond in Japanese yen	Japanese yen issuance will attract international investors; complex mix of green projects means that detailed criteria and thresholds do not yet exist	Alignment with Green Bond Principles

ASEAN = Association for Southeast Asian Nations, US = United States, USD = US dollar.

Source: Authors' compilation.

Key Decision Points

Selecting which is the most appropriate pathway for recognition of a particular green bond and green bond issuer is based on a number of key considerations:

- **Where the bond is being issued.** Are there local or regional regulations or guidelines for green labeling in the jurisdiction where the bond is being issued?
- **Where the projects and assets are located.** Are there specific requirements for green projects in that jurisdiction?
- **Type of investor being targeted.** What sort of recognition is preferred by the targeted investors? Do they have smoother due diligence processes for certified offerings?
- **Currency of the issuance.** Is the issuance in local currency or a G3 currency (i.e., United States dollars, euros, or Japanese yen)? If the issuance is in local currency, are international investors likely to participate?
- **Types of green projects and assets associated with the bond.** Are there criteria or thresholds for the projects and assets? What effort is required by the issuer to meet the criteria or thresholds?

The most appropriate recognition or certification for a green bond depends on how well the green label is received by the potential investors in the green bond. The green label is a marketing tool; therefore, it comes down to what label the customers accept, respect, and desire.

Issuers should discuss these preferences with their existing investors and other advisers to get early guidance on what they should do, and not do, in seeking recognition for their green label.

Media, Stakeholders, Indices, and Listings

Green bonds are debt securities issued by financial, corporate, or public entities where the proceeds are used to finance green projects and assets. They are just like regular vanilla bonds in structure and credit rating. The green label is a bonus feature to the bond from the investor's perspective and a powerful market signal from the issuer's perspective.

The green label for the bond refers to the projects and the assets associated with the green bond, rather than broader green credentials of the issuer. However, any issuer of a green bond is interested in how the issuance will assist its overall marketing efforts.

The green label is also valuable for asset managers, who buy green bonds as a service for investors higher up the investment food chain. Asset managers have a strong interest in demonstrating their green efforts and achievements so that they can further enhance their potential to win new mandates from their investor clients.

Building Momentum

Many organizations are moving to identify and highlight their green and sustainability credentials to their stakeholders. This is a very strong trend in most advanced economies and is growing quickly in emerging and developing economies as well.

The market is seeing a wide variety of sustainability reports and ESG assessments from companies and a determined move toward integrated reporting across financial and nonfinancial outcomes. The use of green financing, through issuing green bonds or buying them, provides reinforcement to an organization's green and sustainability efforts, and hence builds momentum for an organization that is on that journey.

Investors are often the most powerful stakeholder group for an organization. Reflecting green and sustainability ambitions through increased investor engagement, transparency, and labeling is a way to quickly build momentum in this area.

Media Formats and Channels

Green bond issuers are often motivated by the opportunity to attract media attention from their labeled transaction. This may be for capital market-focused media channels or information flows, or for broader media attention outside of the capital market.

Most green bond issuers create media attention through official media releases as well as discussions with relevant media outlets and reporters. Many use social media to amplify the reach of their media efforts.

The media attention that results from a green bond transaction can be used to enhance stakeholder awareness of the issuer's green objectives and achievements.

Index Inclusion

Most green bond index providers currently get their base data from the CBI. The CBI's Green Bond Database has been created over many years and has recently had an update to its methodology.

Many more organizations are creating robust information flows for sustainable finance market players and index providers. As the green bond market matures, there has been a shift from early data sources (e.g., the CBI, which is a nonprofit, nongovernmental organization) in the direction of more established service providers in the capital markets (e.g., Bloomberg).

Index providers have different criteria by which green bonds are included in their indices. Not all green bonds are included, so it is important to understand their criteria and methodologies.

There are at least five major green bond indices currently in place. More are being created as the sustainable finance market diversifies and matures. Each one has a published document available from its website that lays out the detailed approach for compiling the index.

One of the Green Bond Principles working groups produced a report in June 2018, Summary of Green–Social– Sustainable Fixed Income Indices Providers, that provides a structured summary as of the date of publication.

In addition, Solactive has a range of green bond and sustainable finance indices. Box 3 describes the Solactive Green Bond Index and the definition of what is included in its selection pool.

Box 3: Solactive Green Bond Index

Solactive has a range of green bond and sustainable finance indices. The Solactive Green Bond Index has the following definition of what is included in the selection pool, which comprises bonds that fulfill the following conditions:
  a. defined as a green bond by the Climate Bonds Initiative;
  b. amount outstanding of at least $100 million;
  c. time to maturity of at least 6 months; and
  d. excludes inflation-linked bonds, convertible bonds, United States municipal bonds, and asset- or mortgage- backed securities and other structured securities.

Source: Solactive. 2018. Guideline Relating to Solactive Green Bond Index, Version 4.2.

Some indices may include bonds that are not actually labeled as green, particularly when there are unlabeled bonds issued by "green pure-play" companies. This includes examples such as Tesla, which issues bonds but does not label them green although most investors see Tesla as a very green company.

There is an increasing focus on the ESG and climate credentials of bond issuers. These credentials can be boosted by issuing a green bond that is included in market indices.

Listing Platforms

Many stock exchanges and securities exchange platforms around the world are creating green finance and sustainable finance products. This is a growing trend in Asia in particular (Table).

The Sustainable Stock Exchange Initiative has around 100 partner exchanges, of which around 60 have a listing platform for small and medium-sized enterprises, and over 30 have ESG bond segments.

Listing a green bond on one or more exchanges or listing platforms creates greater awareness and increased access for potential investors. For smaller-scale green bonds, being listed can improve liquidity and expand the number of investors who can buy the bond.

Table: United Nations Sustainable Stock Exchange Initiative Members among ASEAN+3 Stock Exchanges

Stock Exchange	Economy
Hong Kong Exchanges and Clearing Limited	People's Republic of China
Shanghai Stock Exchange	People's Republic of China
Shenzhen Stock Exchange	People's Republic of China
Indonesia Stock Exchange	Indonesia
Japan Exchange Group	Japan
Korea Exchange	Republic of Korea
Bursa Malaysia	Malaysia
Philippine Stock Exchange	Philippines
Singapore Exchange	Singapore
Stock Exchange of Thailand	Thailand
Hanoi Stock Exchange	Viet Nam
Ho Chi Minh Stock Exchange	Viet Nam

ASEAN = Association of Southeast Asian Nations.

Note: ASEAN+3 refers to the 10 members of the Association of Southeast Asian Nations plus the People's Republic of China, Japan, and the Republic of Korea.

Source: Sustainable Stock Exchanges Initiatives. http://sseinitiative.org/exchanges-filter-search/#.

Post-Issuance Reporting and Disclosure

Green bond issuers are expected to provide regular reporting to investors and the market after their green bond has been issued. These update reports are important aspects of investor communications and the issuer's green objectives. The format and frequency of the update report will depend on the specific circumstances of the issuer and the relevant bond, loan, or other debt instrument, as well as the program of bond issuances.

Update reports usually contain three different types of reporting, and often the first two types of reporting are combined into the allocations section of the update report:

1. **Allocation reporting.** This confirms the allocation of the bond proceeds to green projects and assets (Figure 18).
2. **Eligibility reporting.** This confirms the characteristics or performance of green projects and assets that support their eligibility to be associated with the green bond (Figure 19).
3. **Impact reporting.** This discloses the metrics or indicators that reflect the expected or actual impact of green projects and assets (Figure 20).

Figure 18: Allocation Reporting

The allocation reporting part of the update report should include the following:

- confirmation that the green bond is aligned with one or more established approaches to labeling, including statements of alignment with other applicable standards such as the Green Bond Principles, the ASEAN Green Bond Standard, the Climate Bonds Standard, domestic regulations in the People's Republic of China, Japanese Green Bond Guidelines, or other approaches;
- a statement on the objectives of the green bond;
- the list of green projects and assets to which proceeds have been allocated (or reallocated);
- the amounts allocated to the green projects and assets;
- an estimate of the share of the green bond proceeds used for financing and refinancing, which green projects and assets have been refinanced, and the look-back period for refinanced projects and assets; and
- the geographical distribution of the green projects and assets.

ASEAN = Association of Southeast Asian Nations.

Source: Authors' compilation.

Figure 19: Eligibility Reporting

The eligibility reporting part of the update report should include the following:

- confirmation that the green projects and assets continue to meet the relevant eligibility requirements that are described in the green bond framework, and
- information on the environmental characteristics or performance of green projects and assets that are relevant to the eligibility requirements.

Source: Authors' compilation.

Some bonds have a very stable allocation of proceeds and do not need to track any performance indicators to maintain the eligibility of the projects and assets (e.g., financing for a single large-scale solar facility). This means that the update report provided by the issuer each year can be very concise and simply restate the information from previous reports.

If there are limits to the amount of detail that can be made available in the update report about specific green projects and assets, then the issuer can provide summary information such as the sectors covered by the green projects and assets, or the regions where they are located.

Figure 20: Impact Reporting

The impact reporting part of the update report (if it covers impact reporting) should include the following:

- expected or actual outcomes or impacts of the green projects and assets with respect to the objectives of the green bond;
- qualitative performance indicators and, where feasible, quantitative performance measures of the outcomes or impacts of the green projects and assets; and
- methods and the key underlying assumptions used in preparation of the performance indicators and metrics.

Source: Authors' compilation.

While impact reporting is strongly encouraged by investors, green bond issuers need to weigh the benefits and costs of the efforts required to track and quantify impacts over the term of the bond.

Reporting Formats and Channels

Green bond issuers provide their information in a wide variety of formats. The information is sometimes included in a broader sustainability report for the organization. The green bond update report is often provided by the issuer as a separate document.

Most green bond issuers provide their green bond documents, including update reports, on a sustainability or green bonds page on their respective website. This enables investors and market analysts to easily access the information on a regular basis.

The timing of providing the update report can be aligned with the issuer's schedule of regular reporting and does not need to follow the anniversary of the issuance of the green bond.

Issuers are encouraged to make the update report available through existing capital market reporting channels such as the issuer's website, stock exchange's information dissemination portal, or local green bond platform. This streamlines the information gathering process for investors and analysts, further strengthening the value of the green label and reducing transaction costs.

Channels for issuer reporting include various market information providers such as *AsianBondsOnline*, Environmental Finance, the CBI, and stock exchanges.

Further Issuance of Labeled Instruments

There is more demand for green bonds and sustainable finance products than there is supply across all geographies, sectors, and ratings bands.

This supply–demand imbalance is likely to continue and perhaps become even more stark. Many cite this supply–demand dynamic as driving the relatively lower funding costs for some green bonds when compared with similar conventional bonds.

Strong Investor Appetite

Investor engagement is a key part of labeling a bond and the increased transparency enjoyed by labeled bond investors is likely to be a lasting shift resulting from the rise of green, social, and sustainable bonds.

Many issuers of green bonds have found that they have much more market power in their labeled transactions compared to normal issuance dynamics. Some have used investor selection processes to assist with aligning issuance distributions with investor credentials.

Some green bond issuers have benefited from reverse inquiries from investors who are looking to provide capital to the issuer outside of the defined bond issuance transactions, with resulting low transaction costs for the issuer.

Green, Social, and Sustainable Portfolios

Most investors in green bonds also have mandates to invest in bonds labeled as social or sustainable. Investors are very encouraging of issuers to explore these other labels as well.

There is important guidance available on labeling bonds as either social or sustainable, similar to the use of the Green Bond Principles for green labeling, based on the Social Bond Principles and the Sustainable Bond Guidelines available on the International Capital Market Association website.

Many governments have a wide variety of projects, assets, and expenditures that cover a broader range of priorities than just environmental aspects (i.e., green). A broader labeling regime—including green, social, and sustainable projects, assets, and expenditures—has been successfully used by a variety of government issuers.

Tracking the Stacks

Many green bond issuers have large portfolios of green projects, assets, and expenditures, and they will issue multiple green bonds (or green loans) over time.

When tracking the net proceeds from the green bonds and the value of the green projects, assets, and expenditures, most issuers have two stacks in their tracking system (Figure 21). This is to ensure that the total value of the green projects, assets, and expenditures is always more than the total outstanding value of the green bonds issued.

Some issuers will allocate specific projects, assets, and expenditures to particular green bonds, while other issuers will look at the broader portfolio of green projects, assets, and expenditures as a single piece.

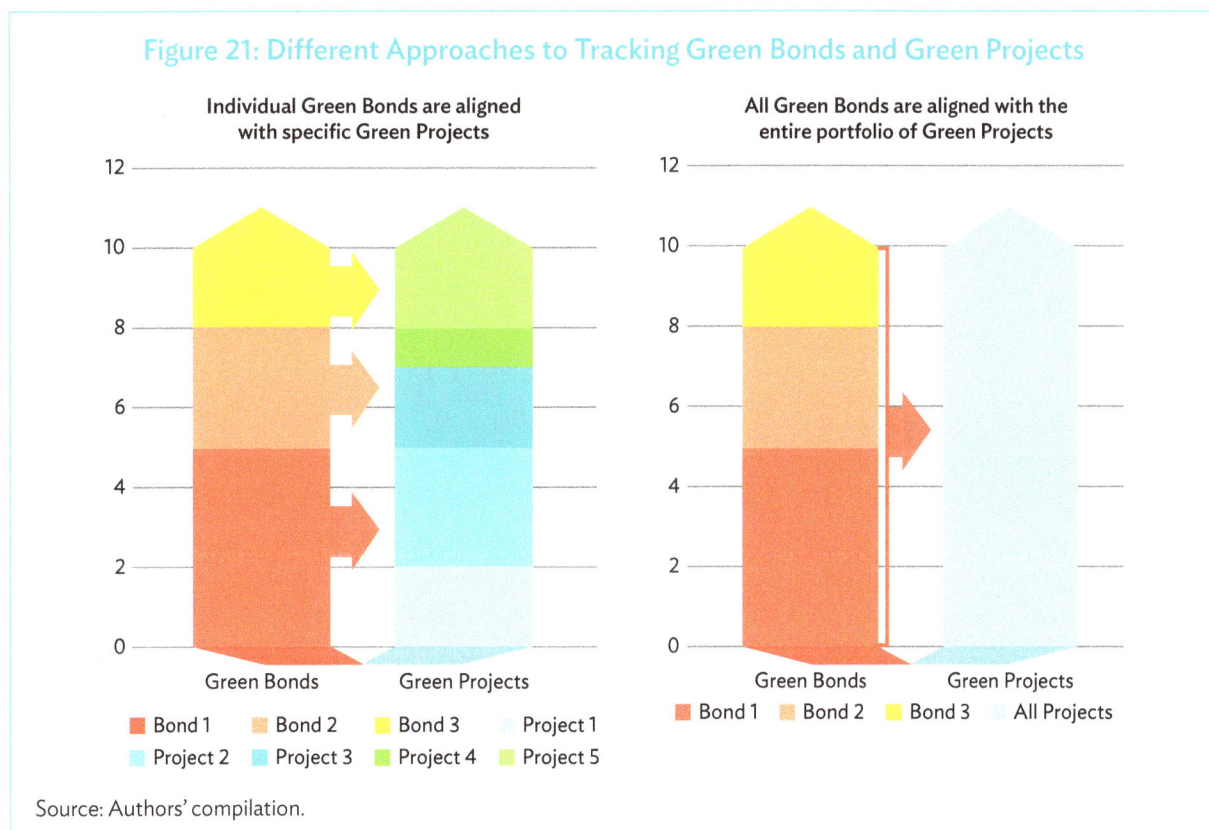

Figure 21: Different Approaches to Tracking Green Bonds and Green Projects

Source: Authors' compilation.

Efficiencies and Transaction Costs

As described in the overview, the first green bond issuance is challenging for most issuers but worth the effort. Following an initial issuance, the vast majority of green bond issuers say that they will definitely issue another green bond.

Issuers that present a program of green bonds (or other labeled instruments) are inherently more attractive to investors, as they hold the prospect of reduced due diligence for future transactions.

The costs and resources required to establish the necessary frameworks and internal processes are generally front-loaded, meaning that the effort required for the second green bond is substantially less than for the first, while the effort for the third is less than for the second, and so on. As further green issuance occurs, the extra effort from the issuer for labeling continues to decline.

The Climate Bonds Standard includes a formal approach to this situation called "programmatic certification." This streamlined approach is being used by a variety of frequent issuers in the green bond market.

www.ingramcontent.com/pod-product-compliance
Lightning Source LLC
Chambersburg PA
CBHW042035220326
41599CB00045BA/7422